THE
INSECURE
KING

10 Powerful Lessons
from the Life of King Saul

JOHN S. CALHOUN

Published by Argyle Fox Publishing
argylefoxpublishing.com

ISBN 978-1-953259-16-5 (Paperback)
ISBN 978-1-953259-15-8 (Hardcover)
ISBN 978-1-953259-14-1 (Ebook)

ARGYLE FOX
PUBLISHING

Table of Contents

Dedication

THIS BOOK IS dedicated to my lead pastor and mentor, Bryan Briggs. His leadership and friendship have given me a new visual of what leadership could look like: humble and confident.

For some, humility is a distorted thing that causes leaders to think less of ourselves. So we put ourselves down and refuse to accept encouragement and praise for faithfully using the gifts God gives us.

The longer I follow Jesus, the more I realize that true humility doesn't make me think less of me. It just makes me think of myself less.

True leadership doesn't end with humility. A godly leader must also be confident.

No apologies should be given for the incredible gifts God has given you. There's no reason to shy away from your gifts and design. Your gifts are reasons to rejoice and be confident that God designed you. They are fingerprints of God's hand on you. Just remember that your confidence is not based on your greatness. Rather, it's founded on the greatness of the one who designed you and is shaping you into the best version of yourself.

Don't forget that your gift on its own is not sufficient.

You need other believers. And your weaknesses were made to keep you humble and remind you to build a team.

During a dark time in my life, Pastor Bryan reminded me that God doesn't make mistakes. God designed you and me to be kings and queens inside his kingdom. Let's not, then, wear peasant's garb.

Be Confident. Be Humble. Be You.

—John S. Calhoun

INTRODUCTION
Chosen by God

YOU ARE A king or a queen. It might not feel like it, but you have a kingdom. Whether your circle of influence falls inside your family, business, church, or other sphere, that is your kingdom.

Where were you when you received your kingdom? What were you doing?

Currently, I serve as a pastor at Destination, an amazing church in Hopewell, Virginia. I walk into this role every day, confident that God called me to this. But it hasn't always been this way.

When I was called to Destination, I was a manager at our family's body shop in Chester, Virginia. It was a great job that I really enjoyed. It paid the bills and provided a life for my wife and me, but it wasn't what I dreamed about doing with my life.

1 Samuel 9 opens with a man named Saul. At first, he isn't even introduced. The pages actually introduce his dad as a wealthy and influential man. Then we read about Saul. The first thing ever said about Saul is that *"he was the most handsome man in Israel, head and shoulders taller than*

anyone else." That's a good start. Growing up as a short kid, I can really appreciate that.

Saul is a handsome, good-looking guy running an errand. His dad just sent him to chase donkeys. This assignment was far from the dreams God had placed in Saul's heart, but he was being faithful with what he had been given. I'm sure the donkeys were valuable, but if you've ever hung out with one, you know they tend to be stubborn and have a mind of their own. The Bible says that Saul and his servant chased these donkeys for three days. How about you?

I'm not sure what you were doing when you received your kingdom, but it probably wasn't valuable in your eyes. Even now, it may seem like you're in a season doing something beneath you, but this moment is important. There will be times when your future kingdom will demand things from you: decisions, character, and courage that will make you wish you were still chasing donkeys.

Today, will you choose to be content with what God has given you? Will you be faithful with what you have? Even if you're hunting for your dad's donkeys, will you be faithful?

Saul's calling is very similar to most great men and women. They were all doing something that seemed insignificant, and yet they worked hard and allowed the season to grow something in them that empowered their future.

Just before they decided to go home, Saul's hunting companion reminds him that there is a prophet nearby who could help them find the donkeys. That's desperate.

They go to the town, and Saul is welcomed by a moment he could never have expected.

I want to read this for you because there are some who say that Saul was the king that the people wanted, not God. That God gave them what they wanted. 1 Samuel 9:17 reads, *"When Samuel saw Saul, the Lord said, 'That's the man I told you about! He will rule my people.'"*

God chose you. There is no one else he wants in your kingdom. He chose you. You can argue about your worthiness. You can argue about your qualifications. That still doesn't take the calling away. God chose YOU.

Saul walks into what he never could have expected. Samuel, the prophet, has prepared a feast for him and Saul is the guest of honor. The next morning, Saul will be anointed privately as the first king of Israel. Later, he will be anointed publicly, but for this moment, Samuel chooses to anoint him privately so that he will know without the crowds around that God chose him. Saul's response to Samuel in 1 Samuel 9:21 sounds like humility.

"But I'm only from the tribe of Benjamin, the smallest tribe in Israel, and my family is the least important of all the families of that tribe! Why are you talking like this to me?"

In the opening portion of this chapter, we're told that his dad is a *"wealthy and influential man."* Which is true? There's a flaw here. There's shame here. Something's not quite right. Somewhere in Saul's development, he's bought into a lie. This wound has distorted the reality of who he really is and where he came from. This is crucial because we all have a starting point, a place of reference. It's okay if we come from a messed up past, so long as that holds an accurate place in our story. Reality can be your friend if it really is reality.

Samuel ignores Saul's statement. As we look at the life and leadership of King Saul, we'll see how this fundamental flaw crippled his calling, his family, and ultimately, Saul himself.

Instead of commenting on Saul's statement, Samuel walks him into the party where he places Saul at the head of the table and instructs the head chef to bring the finest cut of meat that will be served all night. Then he says to Saul, *"Go ahead and eat it . . . I was saving it for you even before I invited these others!"*

I don't know about you, but I love meat. A good thick cut of rib eye is my favorite. I still remember the first time I stepped foot into a Ruth's Chris Steak House. It was an accident. I was on spring break with a couple of friends from college and we had this crazy idea of driving from Minnesota to Texas for an adventure. There was no agenda, and I still look back and wonder why we went. Regardless, I knew nothing of Ruth's Chris.

We weren't dressed for it but as we had been driving for twelve hours with no air conditioning, we had to have steak. I still remember that day, walking into this amazing steakhouse without a reservation. I was wearing khaki shorts, sandals, and some sort of Hawaiian shirt. My two friends looked no better.

We were escorted to our table. We sat down. We saw

the menu. Yikes! One of us was sick from the drive. Troy, who was clearly out of his mind, ordered soup. Derek's eyes were huge as he looked over the prices. I was living off credit at the time and I thought, "I'm here, let's eat!" I ordered the rib eye and can still remember that choice meat coming to me on a white, sizzling hot plate.

Did you know that when you order steak at Ruth's Chris, it only comes with steak? No veggies. No sides. No nothing. Yeah. Neither did I, and the server didn't warn us. So we ate meat. I still remember that first bite of rib eye. It melted in my mouth. It was beautiful, created just for me, and it was amazing. As I write this, my mouth is watering thinking about my first Ruth's Chris steak. Wow! It only cost me $42 plus tip.

I don't know your story. God does. When he set out to draw the blueprints for your life, he wrote out a book of every good gift he'd give you and every dream he hoped for your life.

Within those blueprints are a set of gifts, talents, and hopes. Those dreams are not your own. God put them there. Those blueprints also contain a set of weaknesses and flaws. These flaws are meant to draw us to our knees and pursue God. We need to realize that these flaws can be a double-edged sword. What can cause us to depend on God can draw out insecurity and shame. We'll get to that in detail later. For now, let's just focus on this one thing.

God planned you. He set dreams in your heart, and he gave you the perfect set of gifts and passions to fulfill those dreams. Those dreams are not yours. They were

God's first, and he is more excited about you fulfilling them than you are.

For now, receive the cut of meat. God has saved the best piece for you. Get the fork and steak knife out because it's time to eat. Don't let it get cold with your indecision. Dig in.

LESSON ONE
Hiding with the Bags

SOME TIME PASSES between the prophet anointing Saul privately and publicly. During that time, the first king of Israel is still overwhelmed that he met the man of God on a three-day journey to find his dad's donkeys. Samuel pours oil over Saul and tells him to go home until the day of his public inauguration.

Although the Bible describes Saul in 1 Samuel 9:2 as *"the most handsome man in Israel, head and shoulders taller than anyone else in the land,"* he doesn't believe it. To him, it is a dream. He thinks he won't amount to much in life, but he receives his invitation to the party like everyone else. It is overwhelming to imagine that God chose him.

Then comes the day. That day, Israel gathers for Samuel to unveil the very first king of Israel. It has been years since the last national leader. Since Joshua led the people into the promised land, Israel has lacked a leader who brought unity to the nation.

In Chapter 10 the stage is set. Everyone is present. Like a scene from *Dancing with the Stars*, all the main players are present as a spotlight shines on the winner.

First, the tribe of Benjamin is selected. Slowly, each family not part of the final selection is removed. The spotlight turns to Saul's family.

Then, something strange happens.

Saul's name is called out, as he's declared Israel's first king. Confetti flies, the band plays, and the party begins as the spotlight turns to where Saul should be standing.

But there's no one there.

Wait? Where is he? This is his moment!

The people are confused. Samuel's like, "What? Where'd he go?"

1 Samuel 10:21–22 reads, *"But when they looked for him, he had disappeared! So they asked the LORD, 'Where is he?'"*

God responds by telling them that Saul is hiding among the baggage.

Hiding?

This is his moment! The spotlight is on! Everyone is looking, waiting, and watching for King Saul! And he's hiding?

What's going on here?

There is a time in every king's life when the king must wait. The king may know that he's meant for something great, but not yet.

This wait is a test in and of itself.

Can you wait? Can you be patient? Can you muster enough self-control to not false start?

The king may know he's meant for something great, but it's not the right time, not yet. At some point, the time of waiting will end. When that time comes, will you step into the role God created for you or will you hide?

Up to this point in Saul's story, there's very little indication that Saul would fail. Everything looks promising. We're even told that *"No one in all Israel is like him."*

But Saul is hiding.

As Saul's story unfolds, the key ingredient that holds him from success has nothing to do with his potential. It has nothing to do with his capabilities. It has to do with shame and his fundamental belief that he is unworthy of the dreams God placed in his heart. Saul's story is sad because it is so similar to many of our stories today.

Most of us fail to succeed because when the time comes to step out into the spotlight, we hide. We're hiding from ourselves. We're hiding from our friends. We're hiding from our God.

Why? Shame and insecurity. Insecurity comes in many forms and shows up in so many ways.

Insecurity insists I'm not worthy.

I'm not worthy of love.

I'm not worthy of acceptance.

I'm not worthy of this moment.

Somehow, God got it wrong.

Shame leads us into insecurity, and it causes us to self-sabotage. We'll talk about this more as King Saul's story unfolds. For now, let's look at you.

God wants to give you a gift. It is your future. It is your most prized possession. It just might be that thing that makes you uniquely you. This gift is your platform, your kingdom. It represents the unique way you'll have an influence and leave a lasting impact on the world.

Open the gift. What's in it? It may be the spouse you

have been waiting and praying for. It may be the family of your dreams. It may be a new business or ministry.

What if you decided you weren't worthy of the gift? That deep down inside, you weren't enough? You're blown away by God's generosity, but it's too big. So you run. You hide.

How do you hide?

We all have our preferred methods. Many are self-destructive: drugs, withdrawal from others, workaholism.

Other forms of hiding are less destructive on the surface but still keep us from God's gift. Our personalities are even formed around them.

Here are some popular forms of hiding.

Busyness. You hide by staying busy, pursuing to-do lists that keep you from your greater purpose. Most people spend their whole lives succeeding in things they weren't created to do. What if you created a stop-doing list so you could focus on what God created you to do?

Perfection. You never finish anything of significance because you have to make everything perfect. Your children don't care that the trip to Disney was perfect. They just care that their dad and mom spent their time and money creating moments for them to enjoy.

Winning. You have to win because it hides those feelings of being less than. Although winning gives you validation, losing causes you to ask tough questions and helps move you to where God wants you to go. Do you have to win?

Criticism. You spend so much time being critical and evaluating others, that you never focus on you. You also fail to see how God is working in others' lives, because they don't measure up to your picture of perfection. Are you writing yourself off as well as others?

Adventure. You're always pursuing your next high and never ground yourself to pursue what you were made for. What if your greatest contribution to the world isn't the next adventure? What if God is calling you to work a boring nine-to-five job, come home after work, and be a good spouse and parent? The greatest investment in tomorrow is a family that loves well today.

Something Else. Take a moment to think about yourself. What is your preferred method of hiding?

For years, my preferred form of hiding has been helping others.

I love serving people, and one of my spiritual gifts is helping. Over the years, serving others has helped many leaders succeed. But it has also distracted me from living out the dreams God gave me. Time is not just something to spend. Time is limited and something meant to invest.

In the movie *The Holiday*, Kate Winslet's character is having dinner with an old movie producer. He asks why she would waste her time with him when she could have any man she wanted. The honest answer is that instead of living her life as the main character in her story, Kate's character chose the role of supporting lady.

Like Kate's character, we all run the risk of settling for a supporting role in the story God is writing.

Friend, it's time to stop hiding.

There are plenty of reasons for hiding. There will always be.

We hide because we're afraid. We're afraid of failure. We're afraid of criticism. We're afraid of being judged as unworthy.

Hiding can actually be the catalyst for your own self-fulfilled prophecy. You hide because you're afraid of not being seen as valuable. The result is invisibility. People never see your true value because you hid it from them.

Let me clarify.

Insecurity is a reality for many who spend time creating a mask that people will accept, love, and celebrate. It's a survival tactic meant to protect your true self. In reality, you present your perceived best self. Then you do everything you can to feed it and protect it, all the while ignoring the real you. The you that needs love, that needs acceptance, that needs people.

For years, I paid so much attention to my mask that the mask created a very real fear inside of me. This fear became crippling. *What if the people who surround and support me don't love and accept the real me?* This mask became a monster that crippled me from showing my true self.

Insecurity is tied to our pride. It's a masked humility. Humility is not thinking less of yourself. It is thinking of yourself less and focusing on helping others out of a genuine desire to see them succeed.

Craig Groeschel has a simple way of ending every leadership podcast. If you have to find a mirror nearby, look yourself in the eye and say two words:

"Be yourself."

Be the you that God created. Be vulnerable. Be real. Aim to be the best version of yourself, and make the decision to throw the mask of insecurity away. You don't need it.

God has made no plans for your false self. He didn't create that. He created the vulnerable and powerful you. That real you is the only one he is interested in. The story he is writing is the one where you become everything you were meant to become and take hold of the dreams he has placed in your heart.

Friend, stop hiding. You are worthy of love. You are worthy of celebration. You are worthy to live the life God has for you.

LESSON TWO
Chasing the Applause

INSECURITY WILL MAKE you lose every time, whether you're a new leader, a seasoned veteran, or somewhere in between.

Maybe you have some wins under your belt or perhaps you're still waiting for the right season. Wherever you find yourself, have you paid attention to the compass that drives your decisions or your money? For some leaders, there's a significant drive to succeed for the sake of success. For others, there's a drive to serve God and people.

There are other drives inside our hearts that we must pay attention to. One is the applause of man. The temptation for popularity is one drive that can derail leaders from living out the dreams God sets in their hearts.

It's not that praise is a bad thing. Actually, the word *encouragement* means "To breathe courage into." Doesn't sound bad, does it? After all, we need people to encourage and challenge us to go faster and further. But it becomes dangerous when the praise becomes the compass that dictates what we do and how we do it.

The praise of man is a fickle thing that will cause leaders to let stupid take over their brains. And stupid will always want to take over your brain.

Stupid will convince you that you're something really special. It will tell you that you can step into situations you shouldn't be in and not get harmed.

When you chase the applause of man or woman, you assume roles you aren't meant to be in, make decisions that don't make sense to anyone, and outright disobey God's commands.

For Satan, the stupid drew out pride. He believed himself worthy of worship and became tired of leading others to worship God.

For Gideon, it drew him to lead his people right back into idol worship instead of back to God.

For myself as a father, the stupid tempts me to lead my children to myself instead of pointing them toward Jesus, their provider and protector.

If you're a leader, this is a big problem. If you're a Christian leader, it will force you to step outside the boundaries of Christian leadership. Because the root of Christian leadership starts and ends with following. The stupid puts that to the side.

Don't believe it? Look at King Saul.

Quite a bit happens after he is anointed king over God's people. He gets some wins behind him. He leads the people to military victory over a nation that was bullying God's people. Samuel says "Goodbye"—not as an influencer, but as Israel's formal leader.

In 1 Samuel 13, Saul prepares to enter into battle

with a nation that will become his lifelong nemesis. He has 30,000 people with him. Standing in the other corner are the Philistines. They're big. They're bad. And they have 30,000 chariots plus another 6,000 horsemen and troops.

The text reads that the Philistine army is *"like the sand on the seashore."* When the Israelites see this huge enemy, they freak. Many of them hide in caves, among the terrain and in tombs. Seriously, you can't get any lower than hiding in a grave.

The people of Israel were commanded that before entering battle, they were to worship God and offer sacrifices. God desires that his people praise him in advance for the victory and seek guidance for battle. In addition, worship reminds them that they are more than what they conquer.

Saul and his troops know God's command to worship first and battle second, but there is a problem. Not just anyone can offer the sacrifice. The prophet (and later the high priest) is the one person designated by God to offer the sacrifice.

So Saul waits. And waits. And waits.

Finally, he can't wait any longer. He's losing soldiers by the minute. He watches them scurry away, hiding anywhere that might offer protection. So Saul takes action.

Rather than waiting for Samuel the prophet, Saul lights the sacrifice.

In leadership, timing is everything. That's why patience is such a huge part of leading people well.

Have you ever rushed the plans God placed in your

heart? God's greatest rescues require patience as a primary ingredient. In Saul's story, we'll never know what miracle God had up his sleeve. Instead, we see a mess caused by fear.

As king, there were very few things Saul couldn't do. Lighting a sacrifice is one of them. And he blows it.

As Samuel approaches the altar, I picture him shaking his head. Saul goes to meet Samuel, ready to offer every excuse, even blaming Samuel for being late. He says something that speaks to a fear of every leader in 1 Samuel 13:11. *"I saw the people were scattering from me."*

There's a fear in the heart of every leader that one day they might turn around and realize no one is following them. It's part of the test of leadership. Leadership is about influencing others, and this fear is valid. For Saul, this was a huge problem. As seven days passed waiting for Samuel, Saul's army of 30,000 dwindled to 600. His team was dropping like flies and fear gripped him. Fear caused Saul to forget that success does not depend on his leadership skills but on his courage to trust the God who wanted to prove his might.

As a leader, you'll make a lot of decisions. Will they be wise?

One of my heroes and greatest mentors in life is my father-in-law, Rick. He loves Jesus and his family. Years ago, while I was pursuing my amazing wife, Rebecca, I recognized that my relationship with my father-in-law wouldn't be normal. He had tons of wisdom and grace and shared it with anyone willing to listen. I was willing.

During one conversation, Rick challenged me to not

get distracted by the noise of ministry and the dangers of popularity. "Helping people will make you feel good," he said. "They will celebrate you for the gifts that God has given you."

Over the years, I've grown to recognize that my greatest challenges as a leader won't come from making decisions or solving problems. My greatest challenge is remembering what priorities matter most in my life.

As Rick said, "Your greatest ministry and your greatest leadership challenges will always arise within your family."

These words echo the sentiments of Joshua 24:15. *"Choose today who you will serve. . . . As for me and my family, we will serve the Lord."*

As a leader, I want to leave a legacy. I suspect you do too.

Your legacy begins with the people closest to you. Your legacy will be with your partner and how you love them. Your legacy will continue with the children God entrusts to you.

As a dad, I'm learning that children are like plants. They require constant attention. They require feeding, watering, and continual investment. My children are still young and although I've not seen a full return on my investment, I'm beginning to see my efforts pay off.

Parenting reveals internal struggles that aren't easy to deal with. Parenting reveals my own lack of patience, frustration, and even anger when these little humans don't act like they should. Children put their parents' hypocrisy on display. It's so much easier to focus on ministry. I recently confessed this to Rebecca—that it's easy for me to run off to work instead of focusing on the tough work of family.

Ministry allows you to focus on other people's problems and not your own. Ministry also offers instant feedback and gratification. It can feed your ego and cause you to lose focus on what matters most.

I believe this is why God challenges leaders to make their greatest investments in their homes. Once these investments are made, leaders are better prepared to look outward to whatever other opportunities God places in their paths and hearts.

Remember, the crowd may be loud now, but one day the applause will die away. Then you'll recognize that your family needed you most all along. Your children will be the truest measurement of your character.

Our compass will determine the decisions we make. If we choose to walk in pursuit of God, we will choose wise, bold, and God-honoring decisions for our family and our other areas of influence. If we walk in pursuit of the crowd around us, even the motives for those decisions should be called into question.

Insecurity will poison our decisions because we rob the very foundation for making those decisions.

Does this mean that we won't have wins? No. We'll still have wins. The appearance of success can follow us, even with insecurities. Those wins might even be big enough to hold our attention, preventing us from seeing the truth.

Saul was always in battle. This was a hallmark of his leadership. In leadership, winning is not always a clear thing to determine. Perhaps the reason Saul spent so much time at war was because it affirmed his success as a leader.

Do you remember the simple desire to please God— the desire you had when you were called? There was a time when you were so desperate to be used by God that you would have given up everything. You would have sacrificed time, sleep, and popularity to be considered to be useful in God's eyes. Remembering your humble beginnings should sustain you, even when the crowds beg you to give them what they want. Following God's desire is worth it!

The applause of man is alluring. Don't cave. Don't think so little of yourself that God doesn't see you.

In Galatians 1:1, Paul calls himself an apostle, *"not from men nor through man, but through Jesus Christ and God."* He then asks a significant question in verse 10: *"Am I now seeking the approval of man, or of God? Or am I still trying to please man? If I were still trying to please man, I would not be a servant of Christ."*

It's not that the titles of man aren't fun. It's not that they are not valuable. But what do you want? Choose today whom you will serve. As a leader, you might get a choice, but as a Christian leader, you don't get a pass. Will you be a servant of man or of Christ?

I beg you to choose God's kingdom. Although his kingdom is not currently as loud as man's praise, his kingdom will last an eternity and his rewards are far more valuable than any reward man can give you.

LESSON THREE
An Irrational Vow

SOMETIMES A TITLE comes with a written job description. Sometimes it doesn't. Regardless, titles can be dangerous when they cause you to have unrealistic or unreasonable expectations.

The more I read about leadership and actually lead, the more I realize that leadership is about moving people to take next steps that are better for their reality, not mine.

One leader of the early church, Peter, tells his audience in 1 Peter 2:17, *"Fear God and honor the king."* In our culture, honor is a difficult thing to come by. In our modern society, we equate honor with respect.

I recently heard a young wife say, "When my husband does something worthy of respect, I'll show him respect." Although I agree that respect should be earned, honor is totally different.

Honor shows great value to someone or something because God said it was valuable. This goes for leaders and governing authorities, including the President of the United States. Honor is a biblical value that requires a choice. Peter's statement may sound warm and fuzzy, but when he wrote it, the king was persecuting and murdering Christians. He was torturing them. Hunting them down.

In the middle of that, Peter tells early followers of Jesus that the king would be held accountable for his choices. Their responsibility was to honor him, regardless of whether or not he honored the true King.

Wait, kings are held accountable?

Leaders, pay attention.

Leaders aren't just voted for and chosen by people. Leaders are appointed by God and are therefore accountable to him. This is the other edge of the sword of honor. Fearing God is not just for normal people. Fearing God is essential for all would-be leaders.

As a leader, I must realize that this kingdom of mine is not mine at all. It is God's. I am entrusted with people, his people, to shepherd as he directs. God expects me to be worthy of being his choice.

Enter Saul.

I challenge you to read all of 1 Samuel 14. In it, Saul's son, Jonathan, set a daring plan in motion to test God with a military victory. He grabs his armor bearer and decides to pick a fight with the enemy. It was a litmus test to determine whether God wanted them to go forward with the fight.

As the scenario plays out, it becomes clear that God will show up in a big way and destroy their enemy. Saul, who is with the rest of the army of Israel, sees what's going on and joins in the fight.

In verse 24, you read that *"the men of Israel were pressed to exhaustion that day, because Saul had placed them under an oath."* The oath was that they would not eat anything until the enemy was destroyed.

On the surface, this oath might not sound like the worst plan ever. It may even sound noble. Except this was a grueling hand-to-hand battle that put an unusual pressure on the army.

Here's the kicker. Saul was clear that this battle wasn't for God. It was for him. Saul's stated agenda was to "have full revenge on my enemies."

As a Christian leader, my number-one agenda is to pursue God's kingdom, not mine. As a leader, I'm tempted to pursue my will and work toward my agenda. I even enlist "troops" who are willing to help me in those endeavors.

Power can be a dangerous thing. Lord Acton, a 19th-century British politician, is best known for a crucial statement about power. "Power tends to corrupt," he said, "and absolute power corrupts absolutely. Great men are almost always bad men."

In Saul's moment, power employs his hunger to destroy the enemy. But something much worse happens. His own troops became blood-thirsty and sin before God.

On the surface, Saul wins. But it's actually chalked up as a loss. Because there are subtle repercussions of his choice to *"destroy his enemies."*

God set up honor to be a godly response to authority. If you're a leader, you have influence and authority to make decisions. Just as those under your leadership should honor your authority, it is essential that you understand the great responsibility you hold as a leader.

To keep this responsibility at the forefront of my actions and heart, I ask myself a handful of questions. I encourage you to use them as well.

Am I making it easier for people to follow Jesus or more difficult?

Am I making myself more or less available to people who are struggling?

Am I pursuing God's agenda for my ministry or my own?

Am I leading people by my godly example or am I driving them to meet demands?

The more Saul's story unfolds, the more it resembles a cattle driver. Cattle drivers prod and push their herd from point A to point B. Their goal is speed. Their goal is for personal gain. However, read what Peter writes in 1 Peter 5:1–3:

> *I appeal to you: care for the flock that God has entrusted to you. Watch over it willingly, not grudgingly, not for what you will get out of it, but because you are eager to serve God. Don't lord it over the people assigned to your care, but lead them by your own good example.*

As a leader, I've been tempted many times to challenge people to get in line. It's easy to assume that people don't care about God's hopes and dreams for their lives. Our people should be comforted in our presence. But in the middle of doing what I'm asked to do, I can forget that my main priority is to love and value people.

I recently called a few volunteer team members who had gone missing in action. In one of the conversations, I was struck by how necessary it is that we lead our people well.

In response to my missed call, one woman texted me :

Thanks for reaching out. Didn't think anyone would notice I hadn't been around. It's so crazy that you called because I had just been thinking about how I didn't feel like anyone at church really cared about who I even was.

It's important that we see people. It's important that we be leaders who love people well. People are more valuable than what they do for you. Yes, they bring great value to you, but they are valuable in God's eyes. This value is based on whose they are, not what they do.

Saul lost sight that the battle was God's to fight and took advantage of the people who were following his leadership. As leaders, we can either leverage people for our agendas or for a greater agenda. When we leverage honor for our kingdom, we undermine the greater cause that God wants to do.

They aren't your people. They are God's people. Lead them well.

LESSON FOUR
Disobedience

DISOBEDIENCE DOESN'T ALWAYS look like rebellion. My first serving job was at a Tex-Mex restaurant during college, and I still remember one of the first complaints a customer lobbed at me. I did everything I could to please this table. But it wasn't enough. Whatever I did wasn't fast enough, good enough, or hot enough. It was a family of four and regardless of everything I did, I couldn't make them happy. I even tried the line, "This is my first week." Usually people would give that sad look and say something like, "Ahhh isn't that sweet, he is just learning, it's not like he is totally incompetent."

Like many people, I like to be liked. As a result, I wasn't satisfied with those customers leaving unhappy. At the same time, I couldn't go to my manager and ask to discount or remove something from their bill. So I did the only thing I had the power to do. I removed the soda from their ticket.

I still remember the first time I did this. As I laid the check on the table, I said, "Hey folks, I'm sorry not everything was perfect, but I just wanted you to know that I took the drinks off the meal. It's not a lot but I wanted you to know that I enjoyed serving you." I'm not sure which reaction got my attention the most, but I got a tip that covered the drinks, which was far more than I expected.

In some twisted way, their response to my "generosity" got my attention. The free soda became a quick fix when I needed to resolve potential conflict or boost my tips. The problem? This sacrifice cost me nothing and was stealing from my boss to benefit me.

In 1 Samuel 15, Saul is given simple instructions. He is commanded by Samuel to go to war against the entire nation of Amalek and to destroy everything.

In following the story of God's people, there are only a select few cities and people that this command was given out to. The two that come to mind are Jericho and Megiddo. These two are considered significant acts of unusual sacrifice to God. They're unusual because they required saying no to the typical style of battle where the winner gets the spoils of war. Winners take all. These battles are to be given to God as a gift. This gift is a reminder that God is king, not me.

Typically in warfare, you go to battle against soldiers, capture prisoners of war, and keep the stuff. This battle looks very different. Although we're not given a lot of details, we are told that this is for settling accounts with the nation for *"opposing Israel when they came from Egypt."*

Saul goes to battle, but they do not destroy everything.

The last time this type of disobedience occurred, a

guy named Achan wanted a side cut of the loot. In the book of Joshua, the people of God are asked to give Jericho to God as the first ten percent of what God would do through giving the people the land. Everyone obeys the command to take nothing for themselves, except Achan. Instead, he robs God of what is his and hides his loot among his own belongings. As a result, Achan and his entire family lose their lives.

Imagine for a moment. The battle is done. The dust settles and the army is cleaning themselves up from a brutal and bloody battle. The next morning, Saul is so impressed with himself that he decides to celebrate himself and the win.

Samuel comes looking for him. He hears and sees things he isn't expecting.

In 1 Samuel 15:13, Saul greets him cheerfully.

"May the Lord bless you . . . I have carried out the Lord's command!'

"Then what is all the bleating of sheep and goats and the lowing of the cattle I hear?' Samuel demanded.

"It's true that the army spared the best of the sheep, goats, and cattle,' Saul admitted. 'But they are going to sacrifice them to the Lord your God. We have destroyed everything else.'"

Disobedience can look like obedience when it's clothed in sacrifice, but it is neither obedience nor sacrifice.

God loves sacrifice. God has chosen sacrifice as a way of showing his great love for us. Here's the difference.

For God, sacrifice involves something that actually costs something.

People love sacrifice because it gains attention. People believe they can manipulate others into believing they are something they are not. Sacrifice in any form doesn't fool God.

The apostle John says in 1 John 2:5, *"But those who obey God's word truly show how completely they love him. That is how we know we are living in him."*

Love is a funny thing. Although passion can be fueled by sacrifice, trust is earned and preserved through obedience.

My wife of nineteen years, Rebecca, loves gifts. This is especially true when the gift is well thought out and communicate value. This past year, I had the opportunity to take her original engagement ring and significantly upgrade it, and I was able to do it without her even knowing it. She loved it! The gift expressed sacrifice, honor, and love. This fueled our passion for each other, and I still look back on giving that gift as a huge moment in our last year.

Trust is a different thing altogether. Though passion is an important part of any marriage relationship, trust is a cornerstone. Trust is the foundation that you build on. I cannot sacrifice my way to trust. Trust is cultivated by choosing to honor Rebecca daily. To live in covenant. To respect her by obeying the vows we have committed to one another. This shows loyalty to us and to what we are building.

Loyalty is a significant value that you discover only

when putting it under pressure.

Back to Saul. At this time, he's caught in the tension of whether or not he will be loyal to God or to himself. Here in this moment, he discovers that he cannot serve God and himself. He cannot choose popularity among his men and honor God through obedience.

You cannot serve two masters.

Kings who win battles are very popular with their men because when you win, you get to keep stuff. Yes, the army gets paid regardless, but winning a battle is like getting a bonus. It's a trophy and a great way to boost morale among men. Kings who burn everything are not popular. So it's understandable that Saul feels he was robbing his men by being obedient to God. It made no sense. After all, every king wants their people to love them. It solidifies their loyalty to them as a provider.

God will often ask you to do things that are not popular with those who are following you. Even if it is good for the people you lead, they don't like the comfort this may cost them. This may be because people overestimate what they currently possess and often underestimate the benefit of what's in front of them.

Many years ago, John Ortberg wrote a fantastic book called *Overcoming Your Shadow Mission*.

In the book, I learned that every person is entrusted with a God-given vision for their discovery and pursuit. In this vision, they will not only discover who God is, they will discover who they are in the adventure. At points in this adventure, there will be opportunities to forfeit this vision for the sake of a side mission, a shadow mission.

This shadow mission is more than just a distraction. This shadow mission is rebellion.

This is why Lucifer's story is so disturbing. The Bible describes him as a worship leader whose worship turned inward in the form of pride. Although he was created with the mission to lead angels in heavenly worship to the King, Lucifer decides he is worthy of that worship. He wants to be king. It is at this moment that his rebellion began.

Are you seeking to please God or win the applause of man?

Are you seeking God's mission or have you gone rogue?

Are you allowing God to write your story or have you taken the pen into your own hands?

Saul's response to Samuel and in the lines that follow are so baffling because they are overwhelmed with self-deception. He is not only lying to Samuel. He lies to himself. He deceives himself.

No one can deceive God.

Samuel's response to Saul in 1 Samuel 15:17 is something we might copy and paste into our own lives as kings.

"Although you may think little of yourself, are you not the leader?"

Throughout history, God has actively sought men and women to be leaders. These leaders are people he entrusts to show his people what to love, how to live, and who to give their loyalty to. He is trusting you to show others a life that is worth giving their hearts to.

Will you follow Jesus humbly?

Will you lead God's people confidently?

"What is more pleasing to the Lord: your burnt offerings and sacrifices or your obedience to his voice? Listen! Obedience is better than sacrifice, and submission is better than offering the fat of rams."

—*1 Samuel 15:22*

As a father of two amazing children, if you ask me what I want most from them, it's simple. I want them to trust me through their obedience. I believe God works in the same way. Our sacrifice may appeal to the audience surrounding us but God desires our loyalty and this begins and ends in obedience.

What if the greatest sacrifice you could offer was your obedience?

The fall of Adam and Eve, found in Genesis 3, offers an inside look at the greatest temptation known to man. They doubted God's intentions for them. Because God created mankind in his image, he gave Adam and Eve wills of their own. Their wills questioned God. These wills led them to disobey the only command God gave.

The natural response of your will is to disobey God. The reward for this rebellion is death. On the other hand, should you and I choose to trust and obey God's will for our lives, his hand of blessing and favor will carry us.

Do you trust him?

Your obedience, as simple or as complex as it may appear, will reveal your heart.

LESSON FIVE
40 Days and 40 Nights

PARALYSIS.

Have you ever felt that? Have you ever felt like you are in the middle of two choices and you're caught in quicksand?

For forty days, every morning and evening, the Philistine champion strutted in front of the Israelite army.
—1 Samuel 17:16

It should have angered him. It should have caused him to go into battle. It should have caused him to rise up and lead his army head on against the enemy who cursed God and taunted his people.

Instead, Saul is in his tent, hiding. Hiding is a common theme for Saul.

It's likely he filled his day with other matters in the kingdom but the truth is, he's hiding.

The number forty is a significant number in the Bible. Every time you read the number forty, it should conjure up two images. The first image is of a season. We all go through different seasons in life, and every season carries a consistent theme. It can be a season of blessing. It can be a season of loss or transition. One of the best things you can do is to define the season you are in. Once a season is defined, it becomes simpler to know how to engage and succeed in that season.

The second image forty days should introduce is testing. In nearly every instance in the Bible where you see the number forty, you see a person going through a time of testing. Although it is mentioned briefly, an enemy of God is taunting God's people for forty days. That's a long time to stare at an enemy.

This single, man-on-man battle happens often in Israel. With treacherous terrain everywhere, armies often find themselves on opposing hills with a significant choice to make. Who will venture into the valley and take on an enemy from a disadvantaged position? To do so would be tactical suicide. In order to avoid a total loss situation, man-on-man combat would be a common tactic of war.

That's why Goliath is the enemy's choice. He is a beast, ready to crush anyone willing to stand and fight on his terms.

Who would step up and fight him?

No one. Both armies stood still for forty days. Stalemate.

Leaders are often faced with daunting tasks. Many times, these missions are impossible until a leader steps up and says, "Let's do this." Whether it's a business or a church, a new or emerging leader is the one who is willing to risk their neck and step out and call their followers to join them. Instead, Saul presents another option.

In 1 Samuel 17:25, the decree goes out,

> *"Have you seen the giant? He comes out each day to defy Israel. The king has offered a huge reward to anyone who kills him. He will give that man one of his daughters for a wife, and the man's entire family will be exempted from paying taxes!"*

When no one will step out.

When no one can see the win.

When no one is willing to fight, somewhere there stands a leader who is willing to step out in faith and stand up for what they believe and fight for what is right.

Saul was not that man. Saul offered a reward. Saul crumbled, and the people waited in fear.

When a leader hides, those who follow do the same thing until someone steps up.

The real leader will always step up.

When was the last time you were asked by God to step up? It may have been in the face of an enemy. It may have been a vision God gave you for a better tomorrow. Whenever it was, how did you respond? Did you step forward or back? Did you hide?

We have a God with huge dreams. Our God is looking for leaders who will take on giants in his name. When the testing comes, how will you respond?

This story is significant because it highlights the beginning of transition for Israel's leadership on a very public level. Because Saul isn't willing to fight, a young man named David steps up. He is willing to fight for

God. The focus of this isn't on how big of an underdog David is. The focus is on a man who is willing to step up and fight in the name of God.

David has no real business there except to deliver some supplies to his brothers, but something he sees and hears angers him. He hasn't allowed forty days of fear and paralysis to grip him. Instead, he gets ticked, and this anger leads him towards danger.

This is where leaders go. They step forward into danger when others hide. It's not that they aren't afraid. It's that failure and paralysis are not options. Leaders go where others are afraid to go and at the end of this day, David emerged as a new leader in Israel.

If you aren't willing to step forward, someone else will. We have a God with huge dreams who is looking for bold men and women who are willing to trust him, willing to go where others aren't willing to go.

It's so critical that we deal with insecurities and step out in faith. If you don't do it, who will?

Someone needs to fight the giant.

Someone needs to take that mountain.

Someone needs to lead.

If you won't do it, God will find someone who will.

You will miss out on your greatest moments just because you didn't move forward.

What if no one follows?

What if no one agrees?

What if I stand alone?

This is one of the greatest tests of leadership. You may feel like you have a lot to lose—and you may. But will you step forward anyway?

Even if you are wrong, people are looking for a leader who is willing to take a chance and dare to do great things.

What do you do when you are paralyzed with indecision? What happens when you get stuck? Although these may seem simplistic, I hope these questions navigate you toward movement.

Be faithful. Sometimes God is silent, and it's important to recognize that when he pauses, we should do the same. As a leader, sometimes you'll feel the necessity to press forward and take the next hill. What if God desires that you pause, take a break and evaluate yourself, your leaders, and your people?

Get feedback. Ask your trusted advisors, "How are we doing?" "Are we fulfilling the mission?" "Are we headed in the right direction?"

Get to your knees. God loves humility. Humility acknowledges that you don't know everything. Humility is admitting that you're stuck. Humility comes with reward. It's the only attribute where God promises to "lift up."

Rediscover what God loves. If you pursue the things that God loves, he will empower you with his blessing and favor. It may be difficult and it may cost you, but following Jesus always has a cost to it. Pursue the things that God loves and you won't have to move. God will move you.

Here's the real issue. We are sometimes so afraid to make a bad decision that we end up making no decision at all. It's far better making a poor decision pursuing the things that God loves most, than making no decision at all.

Make a decision. Then decide to trust in God's power and love.

THE INSECURE KING

*"I can't go in these," he protested to Saul. "I'm not
used to them." So David took them off again.*
                                        —1 Samuel 17:32–39

Before releasing a new leader to take on a new challenge, a king would appoint that person for the challenge.
Saul doesn't go about it this way. Instead he chooses to
offer a reward to anyone willing to go on this suicide
mission. It's bait. But David isn't interested in the reward.
He's angered by this giant who would defy God and his
people.

Is he young? *Yes.*

Inexperienced? *Definitely.*

Naive? *Absolutely.*

He had it right to be angry toward an enemy who
defied God. The conversation between David and Saul
sounds like a child begging his dad to do something the
dad knows is way over his son's head. I get this all the
time from my children.

Ashden, my nine-year-old son, and I had a conversation similar to this the other day. We went fishing, which
involved little more than casting out a worm, watching
the bobber, and drinking IBC root beer while waiting for
something to bite. I would cast the line out and hand him
the fishing pole. Ashden wasn't satisfied with me casting
the line for him.

Ashden: "Dad, let me do it."

"Son, let's just sit here and enjoy the morning."

Ashden: "Dad, I can do it! I've got this!"

I turned my head to see what was going on with

Whose Armor Is This?

"DON'T WORRY ABOUT *this Philistine,*" *David told Saul. "I'll go fight him!"*

"Don't be ridiculous!" Saul replied. "There's no way you can fight this Philistine and possibly win! You're only a boy, and he's been a man of war since his youth."

But David persisted, "I have been taking care of my father's sheep and goats," he said. "When a lion or a bear comes to steal a lamb from the flock, I go after it with a club and rescue the lamb from its mouth. If the anim turns on me, I catch it by the jaw and club it to death have done this to both lions and bears, and I'll do it pagan Philistine, too, for he has defied the armie living God! The Lord who rescued me from the the lion and the bear will rescue me from the

Saul finally consented. "All right, go ahe "And may the Lord be with you!"

Then Saul gave David his own armo met and a coat of mail. David put sword over it, and took a step or t like, for he had never worn such th my own fishing pole, Ashden reeled in his line, took a swig of his root beer, then cast out his line. It was a perfect cast. He was tired of waiting for permission to do something he knew he could do.

The rest of the morning involved a lot of not-so-perfect casts, untangling fishing line, and asking Ashden to watch where he was slinging his pole while ducking to avoid getting hooked. It was a fantastic day but it required me to let go and allow him to learn.

This biblical battle isn't the same thing. Saul is coerced into letting this kid take on a beast of a man. He is for sure an underdog. His one chance is that he has trained himself in slinging, an artillery type of warfare that shepherds often used to keep their distance from a bear or lion attempting to go after the herd.

But Saul isn't focused on that. Saul makes the same assumption that the enemy made, that anyone willing to fight would fight him on his terms. His battle. Hand-to-hand combat.

Throughout history, underdogs have shown that they can win if they choose to fight their adversary on their own terms. Rather than focusing on the strengths of your enemy, it's vital that you focus on your strengths, your skills that undercut the severe advantages of an adversary.

Before David goes out to fight, Saul gives him his armor. In Saul's eyes, this is a gesture of favor. He is offering his strength and protection. It could also be a gesture of desperation. As king, he had the best armor. Why not give it to the young man who was going to be lying dead on the field in half an hour or less?

As a leader, you have developed a set of skills that complement your giftedness and allow you to pursue your passions with confidence. You have developed skill sets that make you fit for going to battle.

One of my greatest mistakes as a leader has been making the assumption that everyone has the capacity to lead the way I do or would want to lead the way I do. For years, I developed others the same way I developed myself. I would put my armor on a young leader.

Some leaders did well. Most of them didn't. Because my armor wasn't made for them.

In developing leaders, there are many basics they can get from books and training classes. The other stuff— the character and skill sets that fit them uniquely—are more custom fit.

God did not create you to lead the way others have.

God did not create new leaders to lead the way you have.

What makes you think your armor fits them?

He created them differently than you.

Have you ever driven through a neighborhood where every house looks the same? It was as if the developer and builder got together and decided that there would only be three types of houses. Sure, they may be different colors, but there would only be a few options beyond the simple layouts offered. It's easy to get lost because every house looks the same in neighborhoods like this.

Developers do this to save money and create a certain feeling in the neighborhood. Is your organization like that? Is everything cookie cutter like that?

Every young leader you have the opportunity to mentor or develop is a gift from God to you, your business, and the world. It's your responsibility to identify and help these leaders develop their giftedness and skills in a way that complements the person God created them to be. God doesn't do cookie-cutter leaders.

Anything short of this is cheap. It's unrealistic and unfair to them and to you.

Saul did it. You'll do it too. But you don't have to. Here's a challenge for you. Next time you feel tempted to put your armor on a young leader, stop and ask yourself, "Why?"

In this moment, David has the courage to stand up to a giant. At the same time, he has the courage to admit that the armor doesn't fit him.

You and I do not have to wear actual armor into the battles we are going into on a daily basis. As leaders, we will take on wounds and get injured in our daily battles and I believe this is how you will develop your armor. Your custom-fit armor was made to provide protection where you have been injured in the past and to help prevent future wounds.

If your armor had to be custom fit to you, why would you expect it to fit any other? Why would you expect and project that future leaders would all be injured in the same place and similar fashion as you? Our wounds are as unique as our personality. We would do well to assume that each new leader will need to be taught how to protect themselves.

One essential that every young leader needs training in is found in Proverbs 4:23. King Solomon encouraged his children to *"guard your heart above all else, for it determines the course of your life."* Perhaps the best way to do this is to acknowledge that God has given you a heart for a reason. This heart is meant to guide your steps and decisions, and we need to treat it wisely. Because the heart is a complex organ that integrates into every part of our lives, it's important that we protect it and fill it with good things.

Physically

You have a physical heart. Your heart isn't just a spiritual reality. It's a physical one. If you're going to take care of your heart, you have to consider how you are caring for it.

Are you eating foods that are contributing to the health or damage of your heart?

Are you exercising your heart in healthy ways or are you stressing it out?

Emotionally

Your heart feels things. It is the center of your emotions. Some of these emotions are simple, some are sinful, and some are just plain complicated.

Are you dealing with your complicated emotions or are you numbing them?

Are you allowing the people closest to you the ability to speak to your heart?

Are the people closest to you healthy for you or toxic?

Spiritually

You have a heart that is meant to connect to God.

Your heart is how you experience God's grace and truth.

Are you dealing with the sin inside of you?

Are you resolving conflict before it turns to bitterness?

Are you doing the tough work of forgiveness?

As we close this chapter, consider the words of Ezekiel 36:26. *"And I will give you a new heart, and I will put a new spirit in you. I will take out your stony, stubborn heart and give you a tender, responsive heart."*

If your heart hurts, it's a good thing. God has gone to great effort and cost to give you a new heart. It's not your heart anymore. It's his. Are you taking good care of the new heart God has given you or have you allowed it to grow numb from unresolved pain?

Is your heart becoming more stubborn to God's voice or more tender?

LESSON SEVEN
Comparison Kills

IF I'VE LEARNED anything over my years in leadership, both in the business world and in ministry, it's that winning involves teaching, empowering, delegating, coaching, and mentoring. The limits are endless. Leadership is about influence and empowering others to succeed. It is essential that we learn to be vulnerable about our own limitations and liabilities, not merely our strengths and wins.

Have you ever worked for someone who you weren't sure wanted you to succeed? Maybe they sent mixed signals or you couldn't tell if they were bipolar. Regardless of the cues or signs, you couldn't tell if they were for you or against you.

That's a scary place to live.

It feels like hell. I remember a time in my ministry when I stepped under a leader's authority and even basic tasks became impossible to do. It was the most difficult ministry season of my life, a time when every bit of my self-control and character was challenged. I was asked to take on a huge project, one that would increase our church's influence far beyond the borders of where we had gone before. The directives were clear. A budget given. The goals made perfect sense.

Then everything shifted.

As every passing week went by, it felt like goals were moved, my focus changed, and my budget disappeared. As a young leader who wanted to win, I felt trapped. With expectations changing every moment, I felt positioned to lose.

As leaders, it's important for those who are following and leading under your influence to know beyond a doubt that you are for them. You want them to win. You trust them. Will you entrust them with merely tasks or responsibilities? Will you trust them to fail?

After David's success on the battlefield, it is clear that there is a young, bold new leader in town. He is green. He knows nothing about leading an army or even a kingdom, but he does know how to make friends and follow instructions.

As a result, two things occur in the life of this young leader. David makes friends with Saul's son, Jonathan. They become best friends with a loyalty that will later withstand incredible pressure and pain. David becomes successful in everything his new employer asks of him. *"So Saul made him a commander over the men of war, an appointment that was welcomed by the people and Saul's officers alike."* (1 Samuel 18:5)

David becomes successful. His king trusts him. He is given new opportunities for leadership and influence and then the nation notices him and begins to celebrate him. Songs are written in his name and became hits in the kingdom, 1 Samuel 18:7 sings, *"Saul has killed his thousands, and David his ten thousands!"*

What an awesome song! It's a victory song! When you are winning, everyone is alive with joy, unless you are stuck in the trap of comparison.

Anger. Jealousy. Fear.

These are the emotions that begin to well up in the King's heart for this new young leader who is gaining such great success under his belt. These emotions are not emotions to be managed. These are emotions that become enemies of your heart and your leadership. These must be destroyed in you, and this is work you must do if you want to grow in God's kingdom.

As a king, what will your response be when the applause turns from you to another? Will you develop and empower new leaders or will you crush them? Will you be for passionate youth or will you tell them to be quiet and sit on the front row?

As Saul's story continues to develop, you see him continually give into his fears and insecurities. As a result, history records him as one who *"raved in his house like a madman."* (1 Samuel 18:10)

What drives Saul to this madness? Comparison.

When you compare yourself to others, everyone loses. When you come out stronger, you lose because you drown in your own pride. When you come out weaker, you lose because your insecurity crushes you. These are just the losses in your corner.

In the other corner, you fail to lead. You react. You

stop influencing. You protect your ego. The would-be leaders of the next generation lose because they have lost a connection that they desperately need to become all they were created to be. Then they lose trust.

When the Bible talks about leadership, it talks of a mutual submission where we fight for each other. Whether it is a marriage relationship or a staff role, there's too much at stake and comparison distorts the vision of who we are fighting for and who we are fighting with.

The comparison game is total madness and everyone loses. The kingdom suffers greatest because God only makes one-of-a-kind masterpieces. He makes no copies, so it's totally unrealistic to compare yourself to another.

In Galatians 6:4, the Apostle Paul said,

Pay careful attention to your own work for then you will get the satisfaction of a job well done, and you won't need to compare yourself to anyone else.

If you pay attention to the role that Saul delegates to David, it is his. Saul places David over the army he once led. Just as Saul sent David into battle against the giant, Goliath, he sends David into battle, while King Saul stays home.

Instead of paying attention to his own work, he compares himself to his young new leader.

It drives him crazy.

To the point of murder.

One day as he's calmed by the musical talent of this new leader, he hurls a spear at him, hoping to strike him.

Will you be a leader who compares yourself to others?

Will you be a leader who empowers or tears people down?

Will you be a leader who helps young leaders win or will you throw spears?

Will young leaders feel they need to wear armor around you, even when not at war?

As Saul's insecurity and leadership continue, you see failure after failure because he abdicates his role as the leader. This paves the road of comparison and fear.

God's desire is to use you. You have two paths before you. With every choice, you can empower or compare. There is little room for both.

If you choose to empower, you will see the kingdom of God multiply under your influence. It will happen in your home, your business, your small group, your church.

If you choose to compare, you will still see the kingdom of God. You will just begin to see it further in the distance. You will see leaders evaporate before your eyes. You will surround yourself with yes-men and yes-women whose goal is to survive and look good in your eyes.

In 1 Corinthians, Paul says there will always be multiple leaders involved in mentoring and leading people. Paul recognized that both he and Apollos were essential in Jesus growing the church there, and he says something crucial to the conversation. In 1 Corinthians 3:6, Paul says, *"Each of us did the work the Lord gave us. I planted the seed in your hearts, and Apollos watered it, but it was God who made it grow."*

Recognize your role as a leader. Stay in your lane and

don't forget that God will bring other leaders to the task who are gifted in totally different ways than you are. This may reveal some of your flaws, but it should highlight how important teamwork is to God's goals for your life and leadership.

In Saul's story, influence makes a huge shift toward this new leader who is now a fugitive, hiding from his once leader and king.

LESSON EIGHT
Chasing Your Successor

As THE FIRST king of Israel, Saul doesn't have a template or mentor to look up to. There has never been a king in Israel and Samuel, the prophet, keeps his distance. The only people he really has to look up to are either the kings around him or his own family.

Our greatest wounds come from those who love us the most. If you look at King Saul and some of the things he says about himself before Samuel anointed him, there is a disconnect between reality and his perception. Saul is from an influential and wealthy family, but he misses it. Psychologists would look at word choice early in Saul's story and recognize shame as a core wound. They could see the failure before it becomes obvious in the story.

Every leader has a wound. We all limp, but the best leaders show off their scars, not their wounds. A scar is evidence of healing.

In Isaiah 26:3, God promises perfect peace to the man or woman who would dare place their hope and fix their thoughts on him. *Perfect peace.* What does that look like? This happens moment by moment as you choose to submit your thoughts, feelings, and moments to God. Following God's way is a huge commitment but it is not like going on a yearly diet and then revisiting it once a month.

I read something the other day that helps with this. Loving people is a choice, one that needs to be revisited every thirty seconds or so. If we are going to love people, even difficult people, we need to look into how we are doing on a moment-by-moment basis. As humans we are used to loving people when it is easy. When they aren't complicated. We do this by trying to seeing people as they are, not as they appear in the moment.

Trusting God is similar. It requires us to revisit our thoughts every thirty seconds. Our thoughts tend to wander, and we need to offer ourselves grace instead of beating ourselves up and giving up.

Saul pushes God away through his sin and refusal to repent. He pushes his mentor away because Samuel challenges him to pursue God's approval as opposed to the praise of man. He pushes the young man David away by trying to skewer him with his spear not once but twice. The only people who surround him are people who have to be there and those who benefit from being yes-men.

Peace is the furthest thing from Saul's heart and mind, let alone God's perfect peace. Over the years, my best example of this is my lead pastor. One of the things he pursues is the peace of God. God's peace will guide your decisions, if you let it. Whether it be a financial decision for the family or launching a church, he always seeks the peace of God.

Will there be some fear, unanswered questions, and conflict along the way? Sure, but the peace of God has a way of clearing up any fog.

Saul is bankrupt in the peace department. Instead, he's left to his emotions, which leads him to chasing a man all over the wilderness instead of focusing on his role as king and shepherd of God's people.

Emotions are a great thermometer, but they make a terrible thermostat.

Emotions are a gift from God and they've always helped me determine if something is wrong or needs adjustment. The gift of frustration is that it makes you pause, evaluate what is wrong, and make a shift in a better direction.

Emotions were not created to direct your paths. Emotions like anger and frustration are not meant to be on your internal executive team.

As a result, Saul wastes his energy chasing David. For the rest of Saul's years as king, he is either at war with the Philistines or being distracted, chasing his protege-turned-fugitive.

Only two of the times are recorded, one of them in 1 Samuel 24.

> *After Saul returned from fighting the Philistines, he was told that David had gone into the wilderness of Engedi. So Saul chose 3,000 elite troops from all Israel and went in search for David and his men near the rocks of the wild goats.*
>
> *—1 Samuel 24:1–2*

As a king or queen in your kingdom, you have lots to do. You have people looking to you for direction. You have questions being asked of you. You have vision and mission to continue to clarify, and you have people to meet with. You have stuff to do!

One of the greatest tools that every king or queen needs is a stop-doing list. You need one. What are some things that are wasting your resources? They may be wasting your financial resources, people resources, or emotional resources. Whatever they are, they are a drain on the vision God has given you.

These verses are exhausting. Saul just leaves a battle. Then he recruits 3,000 of the kingdom's finest warriors, and they start chasing one person. He thinks David was some place. Then they go to a place that doesn't even have a name. Think about it. If you're looking at a map and see *the rocks of the wild goats*, you're a long way from home. Saul has to take a break to relieve himself, and then almost gets killed by the person he is chasing.

Chasing. Saul is *chasing* his successor. He could be *leading* him. He could be empowering and delegating responsibility. Because this young man happens to expose Saul's weaknesses and insecurities, he throws spears at him and runs him off, causes him to become an ally to the Israel's enemies.

Here he is. Alone. Afraid. Angry. Weak.

As a leader, I hope people are drawn to me. I want to be an encouragement. Whether it is five minutes or an hour, I hope every person I encounter is challenged and inspired to want more. I want my leaders to be resourced with everything they need to succeed in their family and in their ministry.

How do you chase people away? We chase people away with our words. We chase people away by disregarding them. We compare them to others. We chase some of our best people away by ignoring opportunities to bless them.

And our weaknesses?

God speaks to that through Paul very simply in 2 Corinthians 12:9. *"My grace is all you need. My power works best in weakness."*

Our weakness is meant to lead us in two directions and neither involve shish kebabs and chasing people out to the *rocks of wild goats.*

Our weakness should cause us to fall to our knees and humble ourselves before our God, asking him to empower us with his strength and his people.

Secondly, our weakness should cause us to surround ourselves with people who will lift us up where we are weak.

Both of these require a vulnerability that Saul has lost long ago. How about you? Who are you vulnerable with? Who have you chosen to be transparent with? I hope you're surrounded by people who don't just say yes to every whim of your creativity. I hope you're surrounded by men and women who love you, appreciate you, and are sold out to the vision God has given you.

All Saul has to do was go home. All he needs to do is stop chasing David and start chasing the purpose God has for him. All Saul has to do is fall to his knees and admit he's wrong. Unfortunately, he chooses to chase people away and waste the precious resources he is entrusted to lead well.

What will you do?

Who do you need to stop chasing?

What vision could you pursue with the energy you are wasting?

LESSON NINE
Drinking Bad Water

HAVE YOU EVER been so thirsty you'd drink anything? Imagine. You are so parched, exhausted, and thirsty that you'd drink murky liquid out of a mud puddle in the middle of a busy intersection . . . with a straw. Yeah, that bad.

At this point, the author of 1 Samuel leaves Saul and turns to David, a man who seeks after God's heart. It's a method of communicating that Saul's influence over God's people and history is shrinking.

Saul, who is about to head into his last battle with an enemy that refuses to quit, is stuck. Looking over the battlefield, he becomes frantic with fear. As part of the preparations for battle, Saul asks God what he should do. In 1 Samuel 28:6, the author writes, *"but the Lord refused to answer him, either by dreams or by sacred lots or by the prophets."*

How desperate are you for the voice of God? To what lengths would you be willing to go in order to pursue his will for your life? Would your desperation cause you to fall to your knees, to humble yourself before him and beg for answers you don't have in yourself?

Have you been that thirsty for the voice of God? Are you dying for just a whisper from him? A reminder that He's still there? During these dark times we often begin to recognize our wrong turns. It's on our knees where we often begin to realize that it is only by God's strength and breath that we have the capacity to live for him.

As a leader, you will reach the end of yourself. You will come to the end of your intelligence, strength, and patience. If it's in your parenting, you'll likely hit that by the end of the day. If it's in your ministry or business, it may be at the end of the week or after you get to the next finish line. I pray that you come to the end of yourself sooner than later. It's at the end of ourselves where we begin to consult God on our greatest life decisions. On our knees is where we often find the greatest clarity and let go of our stubborn selves.

As you seek God, can I offer some direction?

God is more interested in your heart than your success.

Sometimes we create a pace that is not sustainable for us, our families, or our relationship with Jesus. It's a lot easier to feel significant when you're moving than when you are paused. While you are moving and shaking the world for Jesus, how easy is it to take care of your heart? Then why are you moving so quickly?

There's nothing more important than your heart. As leaders we have been commanded in Proverbs 4:23 to *"guard your heart above all else for it determines the course of your life."* Sometimes life's pace is unsuitable to guarding your heart.

For many leaders, the heart says things they don't want to hear. It speaks of wounds in the past that need to be addressed. But you don't want to. Sometimes this comes as a sharp pain, a pain you don't know what to do with. At other times, it comes more as a dull ache that leans towards numbness.

This is why leaders are tempted to pay more attention to their resumes than their hearts. Resumes can offer consolation to hearts that are stuck.

While you're on your knees, why not take the time to listen to your heart? Why not get some experts together and ask the tough questions? Why not go to the one who created your heart and find the healing you've been looking for this whole time?

God is more interested in your holiness than your happiness.

God is definitely interested in your happiness. Don't miss this. God wants joy and happiness to be a part of a fulfilling life.

At the same time, in order to grow us, he needs to grow our capacity to withstand pain and difficulty and to face ourselves.

As a Christian, you need to know that the greatest gift God has given you beyond salvation is the relationship of his Holy Spirit. Why?

For strength, *yes*.

For direction, *absolutely*.

Don't overcomplicate this. God has given you his Holy Spirit to make you holy.

Peter makes this statement in 2 Peter 3:14: *"make every*

effort to be found living peaceful lives that are pure and blameless in his sight."

As Christian leaders, it's hard to get around the fact that God's desire is to help us become more like him. This begins with a heart transplant, and it continues through the companionship of the Holy Spirit. The Holy Spirit has been given to those who trust Jesus with their lives. The Spirit's responsibility is to not only comfort you when you struggle but also to convict you of sin and unhealthy patterns. As you submit your desires and motives to him, the Spirit will prepare you for heaven and help you through today.

(Is it possible to be truly happy without also being holy? No! So when you seek holiness, you are working your way toward your own happiness!)

God is more interested in your attention than granting your wishes.

If I can only get an answer for this challenge.

If I can only get clarity.

If only.

Why do we exist? God created us. God is not our all-powerful genie in the bottle who grants our wishes. While you are on your knees, pause and ask, *How did I get here?*

What is your response when God doesn't answer your request in the way you hoped? Do you pout? Do you turn your back on him? Do you get angry?

Saul is long past this moment of humility. It's a pretty harsh reality when God refuses to answer you. This happens as a result of years and years of moment-by-moment decisions to refuse the voice of God in your life. As a result, Saul becomes bankrupt spiritually, emotionally, and relationally.

The text reads that he got his closest advisors together and then searches for a medium. He hires her and begs her to get Samuel's attention. He needs his advice one more time, and hiring the medium worked! Samuel is conjured up from beyond our reality and his response to Saul's question has an edge of finality to it.

Samuel responds in 1 Samuel 28:16, *"Why ask me, since the Lord has left you and has become your enemy?"*

Pride and insecurity. They hold hands in the same way that humility and confidence do. Pride chooses self as a god. Choosing pride is making a choice to become an enemy of God. It's declaring boldly that I know best and I refuse to accept correction.

You and I are not God. Pride is madness. Choosing this path will always lead to fear. You are drinking bad water. Drinking bad water will make you sick and will poison your heart, your decisions, and your kingdom.

Dig deeper.

In ancient Israel and even today, wells give access to fresh water. If you want to discover a well that nourishes your soul, you need to dig. Humble yourself, get a shovel out, and start digging. The answers you are looking for might not come as you hoped, but you will discover that God loves you. He is more committed to finish the things he has started in your life than you are.

A few years back, I found myself in a desperate

situation that required my attention. The check engine light had gone off in my heart. It demanded that I dig deeper than I had before. This digging required counseling. A good counselor is like a guide who walks back through your past and helps you uncover unhealthy patterns and habits that have brought you to where you are. Over a period of months, I found that looking back offered insight and healing from wounds I covered up just trying to survive my past. Asking a counselor to help was a humbling step for me because I was used to being the one with all the answers.

What step do you need to make in order admit you don't know it all?

What "bad water" do you need to turn away from?

Where are you digging for answers?

What does your shovel look like?

LESSON TEN
One Final Lesson

I HAVE A confession to make. I'm a quitter. In my early twenties, I was working at an incredible church and was on my way to finish up my master's of divinity in record time. I wasn't ready to be a king, but I wanted to be. I was working in youth ministry and should have been content with where God had me.

During that season, I took some critical feedback about a message I gave. I can still hear the words echo, "What a terrible message. He has no stage presence. Don't let him back on stage ever again." It wasn't just the words that cut the deepest. It was the mouth these words came from that struck my heart. These words, alongside being overlooked for a hopeful promotion, sent me on a downward spiral, taking me out of ministry for years. It wasn't a moral failure, but as I look back, I see critical cracks in the foundation of who I was and gaps in who I needed to become.

I became incredibly upset with God as to why my story was not moving in the direction it should be in the particular timing I was looking for. I felt ordinary, and this made me angry. I stepped out of ministry. I quit seminary. If it was going to be this difficult to help God build his kingdom, I was out.

Side note: I don't think God needs us. I believe he invites us to become a part of something he is doing in this world. He invites us to become a part of the greatest redemption story of all time. This begins by looking in the mirror and allowing him to do his greatest work inside you. **This story is not about how you saved the world but of how God did great things inside your world and through your changed heart.**

I think this is why Jesus said in Matthew 6:18, *"I will build my church, all the powers of hell will not conquer it."* Jesus knows that if you and I build the church, it is vulnerable. He also knows that if you and I are the ones taking the credit for it, we are vulnerable to the pride of trying to be superman or superwoman.

As years passed, God brought me back into ministry. Now, I'm convinced that God will empower you to accomplish everything he has placed in your heart to accomplish. I keep hearing people talk about Plan B, but God has no Plan B for your life. God's plans for your life can handle your shortsightedness and even your sin.

He designed you. He created you. He has redeemed you. I love what the author of Hebrews writes in 12:2. *"We do this by fixing our eyes on Jesus, the author and perfecter of faith. . . ."*

The Bible describes Jesus as the author, not just of our faith, but also of our story. The passions and desires flowing through your veins didn't get there by accident.

Every character trait, wound, desire, and flaw was written into your story line for the purpose of bringing glory to God. As you read this, Jesus is poised, ready to write something amazing into your life. Will you submit to his writing?

God will not write your story without your consent. As you read the final chapter of Saul's life, 1 Samuel 31, approach it with a sober sadness. This is a warning of what might happen should you choose to take the pen out of God's hands and write the story of your life.

Saul is in the fight for his life. He is on Mount Gilboa, many of his army slaughtered before the enemy, the Philistines. He and his sons are being closed in on and it's becoming very clear, this battle is over. Saul, knowing what the enemy will do to him should they capture him, turns to his armor bearer and asks him to kill him. He refuses. Saul is left with one final choice. In his final moments, King Saul ends his own life on the slopes of the mountain. Instead of look to God, he chooses to fall on his sword.

Did you ever play king of the mountain as a kid? One person takes the top of a hill and everyone attempts to drag them down, trying to claim to be the king. I'm not sure how your version went but when we played, it involved scrapes, bruises, and a black eye or two. No one lasts on top long when everyone is clawing to be number one.

I'm thankful that I will not be remembered for how my story began. As you survey your own life, I pray that you take the time to stop and evaluate what drives you.

Saul was overwhelmed that God would choose him. I hope you feel that as well. On the same hand, I hope that you choose the path of humility that God has for you.

Like Saul, when we choose pride as our companion, we take the pen out of God's hand and begin to write story lines that were never meant to be written into our lives and in the lives of those who love us most.

Our lives were meant to leave a legacy for others, but God's sovereignty doesn't demand that we choose the path of obedience and submission. If we do choose to submit to his hand, however, he will write a story that is beyond any we could have written.

On the day that Saul took his own life, his three sons died, and all the troops who were with him died. When we forfeit our courage and build our kingdom at the expense of God's, we forfeit the influence that God has gifted us. God's kingdom is far greater than our personal castles, and it's worth submitting to.

Paul had you on his heart when he wrote the words,

And I am certain that God, who began the good work within you, will continue his work until it is finally finished on the day when Christ Jesus returns.

—Philippians 1:6

In these words, there are three significant promises from God.

One: God has begun something in your life, and he intends to finish it. Every great endeavor, from the creation of the world to his rescue plan to save the world to your story, has a finish line. God doesn't start things he does not finish.

Two: God intends to work on you for the rest of your days. This season may seem like he is being quiet. It may even seem like he doesn't care. Don't forget that he's not letting go and he isn't done with you.

Third: God is happy to receive your feedback, but not because he intends on changing his plans. He is a good God and he has good intentions for your life. God loves you. He is proud of you and he has great intentions for your life.

Give him the pen and trust him to cross every *t* and dot every *i*.

CONCLUSION
What Are You Afraid Of?

WHEN I WAS young, my parents sent my brothers and I camping for two or three weeks every summer. During that time, we'd spend time with our cousins and grandparents. It gave us a lot of freedom, and it gave our parents a break, two desperate necessities after a long school year.

While camping, we stayed in a cabin. This cabin had no running water. So every summer, one of our tasks was to dig out a new outhouse. Fun? Not really. Imagine our cabin, in the middle of nowhere, with an outhouse usually fifty or one hundred feet away. No worries—until night-time. This is when my imagination would come alive. In the middle of nowhere, there are no fluorescents, and the moon and stars weren't enough to light up the path to the outhouse. At least once a night, I would have to make that lonely walk to the outhouse. My creative mind would come to life. This creativity, held inside my seven-year old brain, was fueled by fear.

I feared what might jump out of the woods to maul me.

Sometimes it was a mountain lion.

Other times it was a bear.

Whatever the situation, whatever the noise I heard to my left, it came alive with all sorts of possibilities, all ending with me running back to the cabin fearful of whatever image I conjured up in my mind.

What are you afraid of? Are you afraid of the dark? Are you afraid of figments of your own imagination?

If you're a leader, you'll be called out into places where there are blank canvases to be painted. Do you fill these blank canvases with fears or dreams? As a leader, God will call you to scary places, where you can fuel your creativity with images of infinite possibility. What fuels your imagination?

The problem with fear is that it causes you to cower. It causes you to run.

What are you afraid of? Where does anxiety come from?

King Solomon, a very different king from Saul, penned these words, "Fearing _____ is a dangerous trap." Whatever you fear, it's a trap. Yes, I said it. A *trap*.

Trappers are different than hunters. Both aim to kill whatever they are after, but they have different techniques for killing their prey. Both study the paths that their prey take. Both look for prints. But the hunter lies in wait for prey. The trapper has an altogether different technique. The trapper uses a tool called a trap to capture prey. The trapper places the trap on paths that the prey is familiar with, sometimes using bait to lure it.

King Solomon said fear was a trap. The trouble with fear is that it is a trap fueled by our own imagination of the worst possible scenario. It's not a trap based in reality, but in possibility. Our enemy uses it to paralyze his prey, to render him or her helpless. Have you been there?

In King Solomon's case, he recognized that *"fearing people is a dangerous trap."* (Proverbs 16:9a) We can absolutely be afraid of people. Have you ever been afraid of someone? It's crippling. It may have been a bully or someone who just intimidated you. Fearing people is a dangerous trap of the enemy to subdue you.

Fear does far more than paralysis. People end up serving the thing they fear. When it comes to people, we fear their rejection or criticism and never really become the person we were created to be. Instead, we stay wherever we currently are to please whoever we fear.

Fear initiates chaos into our world and it makes us feel powerless, regardless of the truths we hold to with confidence. As I write the closing words of this book, my family is going through the coronavirus quarantine just as you may be. There's fear in the air. People have lost jobs. They have lost loved ones. This virus has spread throughout most of the world, causing a very real chaos in the hearts of men and women alike.

Fear is similar to any virus. It spreads like a wildfire and it causes men and women alike to lose perspective on reality. In the middle of this epidemic, I found myself in Mark 4:35–41, finding incredible reality and truth that applies to the epidemic and to our lives as leaders.

As evening came, Jesus said to his disciples, "Let's cross to the other side of the lake." So they took Jesus in the boat and started out, leaving the crowds behind. But soon a fierce storm came up. High waves were breaking into the boat, and it began to fill with water. Jesus was sleeping at the back of the boat with his head on a cushion. The disciples woke him up, shouting, "Teacher, don't you care that we're going to drown?" When Jesus woke up, he rebuked the wind and said the waves, "Silence! Be still!" Suddenly the wind stopped, and there was a great calm. Then he asked them, "Why are you afraid? Do you still have no faith?" The disciples were absolutely terrified. "Who is this man?" they asked each other. "Even the wind and waves obey him!"

As a leader and a follower of Christ, you will go through storms simply because Jesus asked you to go to the other side of the lake. Jesus will put you in that awkward position. As you read the next section, Jesus only had one appointment on the other side of the lake. Then they get back in the boat and go back. Jesus will spare no expense in pursuing one vision, one agenda, one person. You and I must remind ourselves that it is worth it. If it's worth the expense and the pain to Jesus, it should be worth it for you and me.

Another incredible truth is simply this. If Jesus is in your boat, you're in good company. If he's asleep and not worried, you and I have nothing to be worried about. There may be a storm around you, but the storm doesn't have to get inside of you. Know that God is in control, even when you realize you are not.

"Why are you afraid?"

This is a crucial question. You may call it a rebuke. As I read it, I think it's a significant question. When I'm afraid, it's often because of loss of control. It's because I can't turn off the storm. You and I need to know that we are not in control. As a king or a queen, we will often feel we are building something amazing for God. The truth of the matter is that God will put you in situations that are totally out of your control for no other reason but to remind you to let go and allow God to do what he does best.

Jesus is the best rescuer. He's the best healer. He's the one worthy of our attention, worship, and faith. Do you trust him?

A year ago I was on a charter bus headed to Washington D.C. to visit the Bible Museum after it opened. On the ride, I had the fortunate opportunity to sit with Rabbi Paul Klassen. Rabbi Paul is a messianic Jew who has become a huge friend and mentor to our team at Destination Church. As we talked, we got into a conversation about the true meaning of the Jewish word *shalom*.

Sometimes when words get translated to English, they lose their meaning. *Shalom* often gets translated into a greeting or a goodbye. It is translated in most English bibles as peace. As we were talking, it became apparent to me that *shalom* carries much significance that I hope you'll allow to be embedded into your spirit. This is what I remember from our conversation.

To the Jewish audience, large bodies of water such as

the Red Sea, the Sea of Galilee, and the Mediterranean were symbols of chaos. Because you couldn't see the bottom and because they weren't flowing bodies of water, they were simply viewed as bottomless pits to the unknown. When God split the Red Sea through Moses, this miracle was amazing. It was as if God wanted to send a message to his people that he would *split the chaos* for them.

Consider this. In the gospel accounts, the first disciples were fishermen. They were hard workers accustomed to taking their boats into unknown territory, into chaos. Is it possible that this was why Jesus chose them? They were comfortable with being on top of chaos.

If this is why Jesus chose them, the storm in Mark 4 was hugely significant. These fishermen were used to storms. For them to paddle and fight against it and come to realize they were powerless against it was huge. You know the rest of the story, but when Jesus speaks peace over the storms in our lives, his agenda isn't to just clean up the mess and give us a warm and fuzzy feeling. Shalom properly translated mean to *"crush the chaos,"* and this is exactly what Jesus does in this moment.

Friend, wherever the fear generates from, God wants to crush that chaos in your heart. It may be generated from outside of you. You may fear your boss or your audience or the vision God has given you. It may be generated from inside of you as insecurity. You may not feel worthy or enough, just like Saul.

Don't let fear become a compass that you use to calculate how you will live.

Fear of conflict will cripple you.

Fear of rejection will destroy your faith.

Fear of being invisible will cause you to settle for the applause of man.

What are you afraid of?

Solomon ended this statement with the antidote for fear, "but trusting the Lord means safety." (Proverbs 16:9b) Who are you trusting? Where does your confidence rest?

The antidote to fear is trust, but what will you choose to trust?

In the dark.

In the unknown.

In the chaos that surrounds you.

In between the reality that God is painting for us to live, we have a choice.

Will you choose to step forward in trust or will you cower in fear?

Psalm 23 offers great guidance for the fear. Solomon's dad, David, declares his dependence on the one he trusted in verse 1: *"The Lord is my shepherd, I have everything I need."* There is a calm that cuts through any potential threat or fear. David is familiar with the dark. He is familiar with sitting in silence wondering what his future might hold. He is familiar with the quiet and the fear that has the potential to grip. For him, there are plenty of things to fear. However, he trusts something bigger than his fears. He places his confidence in God.

"Even when I walk through the darkest valley, I will not be afraid, for you are close beside me." (Psalm 23:4)

It isn't even that he trusts God is going to (fill in the blank). David has a quiet confidence that having God close by is enough.

Our lives display what we really believe about God. What does your life say about you?

What dark valley do you need to walk through? Will you go alone or will God be your companion?

You are worthy of the kingdom God has for you. Will you take hold of the gift and be faithful? The choice is up to you.

Choose to be bold.

Choose to receive.

Choose to live the life God dreamed of when he created you.

Choose today to let God be the author.

Note to the Reader

ONE OF MY favorite things as a pastor, leader, and friend is to grab a cup of coffee and hear stories. As I was in the process of writing this book, I thought about you. I prayed for you and tried to imagine what it would look like to sit across the table and hear your story.

Whether you read this in one sitting or a chapter at a time, my prayer is that you would find encouragement. I cannot begin to guess what God's intentions are in your story, but I am confident that God does not make mistakes.

We are all insecure kings. If you are looking for encouragement, want to offer feedback, or want to share your story, I encourage you to reach out to me at theinsecureking@gmail.com. I would be honored to be a part of your story.

Your story matters. You may be in a season of incredible blessing. Or you may also be experiencing a season of loss or transition. Wherever your story, remember that God is not done. He is not done with your story, and he is definitely not done with you.

—John S. Calhoun